For Mary & Milford
Romanoff
Love,
Ann McGovern
3/3/94

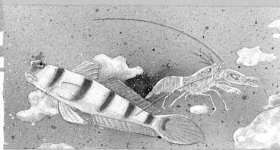

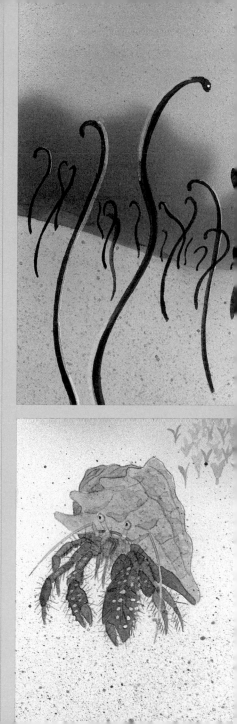

THE DESERT BENEATH THE SEA

By
Ann McGovern
and Eugenie Clark

Illustrated by
Craig Phillips

SCHOLASTIC INC. / New York

Library of Congress Cataloging-in-Publication Data

McGovern, Ann.
The desert beneath the sea.

Summary: Introduces some of the creatures that live on the bottom
of the sea, discusses how scientists study these animals,
and describes an underwater expedition in the Caribbean.
1. Marine fauna—Juvenile literature.
2. Marine fishes—Juvenile literature. 3. Benthos—Juvenile literature.
[1. Marine animals. 2. Fishes. 3. Underwater exploration]
I. Clark, Eugenie.   II. Phillips, Craig, 1922-   ill.   III. Title.
QL122.2.M38   1991   591.92   89-70001

ISBN 0-590-42638-9

12 11 10 9 8 7 6 5 4 3 2   2 3 4 5 6/9

Printed in the U.S.A.   36

First Scholastic printing, September 1991

Designed by Anna DiVito

The artwork in this book was done in watercolor and pencil.

To my newest son and daughter:
John Mulligan and Odile Long Scheiner
—AM

To the three Davids of our undersea desert:
Doubilet, Fridman, and Shen
—EC

To my wife, Fanny
—CP

We could not have told this story without the help of wonderful divers who worked with us for over 20 years. David Fridman shared his immense knowledge of the sea's sand creatures. David Doubilet, David Shen, Nick Caloyianis, Clarita Berger, Ruth Petzold, Ed Bunyan, Jr., and Ian Murdock photographically documented the scientific and exquisite nature of our sand creatures.

Many other scuba divers helped us in discovering and adding new knowledge and information. We thank the students from the Department of Zoology at the University of Maryland: Phyllis Anastos, Stella Chao, Carol Falck, Anita George, Cheryl Goldberg, Daphna Herold, Steve Kogge, Marianne Krall, Karen Moody, Simon Nemtzov, Jennifer Nunes, Vicki Rasey, Lisa Volgenau, and Joshua Wilkenfield. Divers from all swims of life who especially helped us are: Tom Alburn, Linda Benveniste, Don Blair, Gloria Borer, Laird and Bitsy Bryson, Joe Cozzi, Rouby Deuvletian, Lillian Hoffman, Sue Holderman, Ruth Jacobson, Ray Jarvis, Ginny and Ben Kendall, Ivi Kimmel, Martha Kiser, Niki and Hera Konstantinou, Bob Korth, Betty Ann Llewellyn, Mike McDowell, Maya Moltzer, Amos Nachoum, Penny Pemberton, Mary and John Pohle, Joan Rabin, Leonore Reich, Howard Rosenstein, Dee Scarr, Marty Scheiner, Naomi Stern, Mary Jane Stohl, Linda Sweeting, Ayman Taher, Edith Taylor, Helen Vanderbilt, Gail Weinmann, and Lucy Breathitt. We thank them all for hardworking and fun diving days together.

Contents

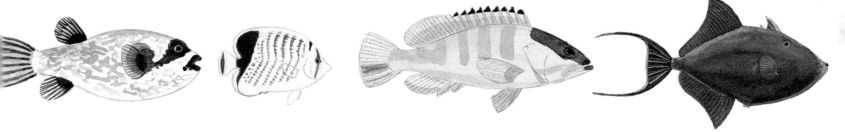

1. Come to the Desert Beneath the Sea

You are gliding underwater, a scuba tank on your back. You are weightless as you float along the coral reef. You marvel at the colorful corals and fish in every rainbow hue.

Then you move away from the reef and swim to the shallow sandy bottom, to the desert beneath the sea.

At first, you see only barren sand, dappled by sunlight. Everywhere you look, the sand seems empty of life. Gone are the colorful corals and fishes.

You look carefully at this desert beneath the sea. You see a small pointed pebble. Wait. The pebble is really a nose with a round eye on either side of it, looking at you.

Out of the corner of your eye, you see something moving in the sand. You look up to see a tail of a pale fish disappearing into the sand. You look again. There are hundreds of these fishes in the distance. And next to where you saw the pale tail disappear are many noses and eyes looking at you.

Grains of sand jump in a wild dance. Under the sand grains are tiny, tiny creatures.

The sandy area that had seemed so empty only moments before is really a world teeming with life.

In the open sand, the creatures of the undersea desert are exposed to danger. They must find ways to hide from their enemies.

Some creatures fool their enemies by camouflage — skillfully blending against the background they match. Other creatures whoosh down deep into the sand. Some fish wriggle backwards into the sand. Some wriggle sideways. Certain creatures stay just below the top of the sand.

How do you know they are there? You must take the time to stop and train your eyes to notice telltale signs.

This is a book about the desert beneath the sea and how scientists study the creatures that live there.

But it is also the story of a great friendship that grew between two people who love nature. Ann McGovern introduced Eugenie Clark to the joys of writing for children. Eugenie introduced Ann to the wonders of the desert beneath the sea. We hope you like our story about these fascinating creatures we have grown to love.

2. How Marine Biologists Study the Undersea Desert

Marine biologist Eugenie Clark is known as the Shark Lady. She studies sharks all over the world. But she is also interested in the tiny creatures who live in the desert beneath the sea.

A scientist like Eugenie Clark studies fish in many different ways. As a young girl, she studied fish in an aquarium at home. Now she goes on expeditions to observe the creatures in their homes in the sea. She goes scuba diving to study their behavior firsthand. Many people enjoy diving with her — students, her grown children, other scientists and diving friends, including author Ann McGovern.

Eugenie and Ann have a lot of fun on these expeditions. But they work hard, too.

They learn to lie quietly on the sea bottom, careful not to disturb the creatures they are studying.

Ann takes notes for her books and Eugenie records her findings. They write with a pencil tied to a plastic slate or on special underwater paper held to a clipboard with two rubber bands.

Eugenie and her scuba-diving friends watch how the creatures behave . . . how they act alone and with other sand dwellers . . . how they fight, feed, and mate . . . how the seasons and the sun and moon and currents affect them. They study the creatures at sunrise, at dusk, and in the dark of night.

Eugenie also studies the kind of water and sand in which the creatures live. She spends many hours in libraries and museums all over the world. She reads information by other scientists.

Back in her lab at the University of Maryland where she is a professor of Zoology, Eugenie does further study. She examines fish preserved in alcohol by *dissecting*, or cutting them open. She studies tiny parts of them under microscopes.

She counts the rays in each fin and the scales on their bodies. She measures many parts of the fish.

She examines what remains in the fishes' stomachs to find out what they eat. Sometimes she has to play detective. From only a few fish scales or bones, she tries to figure out the kind of food that was eaten.

In a notebook, she records all her information, called *data*. This data can also be put into a computer, revealing other fish facts. As she writes her findings, she analyzes and studies the computer images.

Her data is published in scientific magazines and books for other scientists to read. Sometimes she writes for popular magazines, like *National Geographic*. Her stories are illustrated with beautiful photographs.

3. If You Joined an Underwater Expedition

Suppose you were a scuba diver and were invited to take part in an underwater study. You would be one of fourteen people — including Ann McGovern — who volunteered to live on a dive boat for a week to study the sand tilefish of the Caribbean Sea.

The leaders of the expedition — Eugenie Clark and Joan Rabin — would give you jobs to do. You would help them try to find answers to many questions about the sand tilefish.

How deep down do these fish build their burrows? What are they made of? Does each fish build its burrow alone or with other tilefishes? Why are the tops of burrows built so big? Is it to show off? Is it to build an artificial reef to attract their food?

Coral reefs around the world are being damaged in shallow waters where people drop their trash — sometimes right in the tilefish's territory. How does the tilefish react to this?

Your first job would be to scuba dive to locate the sand tilefish. Its pale color makes it hard to spot when it hovers above the sandy bottom. You would learn to tell males from females. Males are larger and develop streamers on their tails. They behave differently from females.

Tilefish homes, called *burrows,* are easy to locate because of the mountains of coral rubble piled on top. Some of them are over eight feet across. Juvenile tilefish build small burrows. Once you find a burrow, you mark it with a plastic marker with your initials and a number. All week, you would study that area and the tilefish that live there. You would see that only one tilefish lives in each burrow.

You would measure the size of the roof mounds and the distances between them. You use a compass and a cotton string that is knotted in measured lengths. After each scuba dive, you give your information to Eugenie or Joan. They record your observations in a scientific way. They make detailed drawings and maps of the whole area. Your observations would be part of a scientific study.

Another job would be to help Joan *excavate,* or take apart, a large roof mound. These are made mostly of pieces of broken coral. A tilefish can easily build its burrow and roof mound again.

First Joan divides the large mound into four parts with her diving knife, the way you might divide a pie. One quarter, or *quadrant,* would be studied. You pick up the coral pieces carefully and put them into your collecting bag. When the bag is filled, a lift bag is inflated to bring the heavy rubble up to the boat.

The coral rubble is weighed and sorted. You would work on the back deck, sorting the hundreds of coral rubble pieces by size and shape and texture. The job might take all afternoon. Your back would get very tired, bending over the piles of rubble on the deck. Mixed in with the coral rubble, you might find surprises — fish teeth, bits of glass, and other trash.

A photographer takes pictures of the tilefish underwater. Now he photographs the rubble on the deck.

You would learn many things on this expedition. You would see tilefish at different depths — from eight feet to 168 feet! You would see groups of little yellowhead jawfish that make their burrows nearby. You might wonder why the jawfish live so close to the tilefish. Scientists wonder, too — but no one has been able to come up with a scientific reason, so far.

On many dives, you would see a tilefish pick up a piece of coral in its mouth. It would swim up to a big mound. Yet the tilefish makes its mound even bigger by adding another piece of coral on top! Scientists are still investigating the reasons why tilefish keep building.

At sunset, divers watch the sand tilefish mating. The fish loop and crisscross over one another. Then they swim upward together to release their eggs and sperm that will join to become baby tilefish in a few days.

Divers check up on the fish at night, too. When the sun sets, the tilefish cover the openings to their burrows by fanning the sand with their tails. Then they dive through the soft, new sand that closes over them. Here they sleep until morning, protected from danger.

Joan and Eugenie want to see what happens if a burrow entrance is blocked. They ask you to help. Tilefish move objects by carrying them or dragging them with their mouths. At the entrance of one burrow, you place a red plastic checker. At the second, you block the entrance with a golf ball. You put a clothespin in front of the last burrow.

You watch to see if the tilefish moves them. The red checker doesn't completely block the entrance so the tilefish simply ignores it and slips in and out of the burrow.

The golf ball is too round and smooth for the tilefish to get hold of in its mouth, so it does not use that burrow opening again.

And the clothespin? The tilefish can pick it up easily and move it to the top of its burrow.

Probably the most important fact you would learn is that sand tilefish can make a home out of almost anything. If there is no coral around, they use pieces of a light bulb, parts of shipwrecks, bits of glass, a fishnet or a clothespin — even little pieces of diving equipment. They seem to use anything that might have dropped into the sea.

Sometimes sand tilefish make their home in plastic pipes or under wooden boards that are lying on the sandy bottom. It seems they can live in almost any kind of shelter.

4. Fish That Dive Into Sand

One summer, Eugenie made grids of string on the sand. She marked off a huge area where eleven male razorfish lived with thirty-four females. One male had six females in his "harem."

She noted that each male razorfish guarded its own territory and wouldn't let the other males near. Each male shared its territory with a "harem" of females at night.

When danger was near, the male razorfish dived into the sand. It always chose the same spot in the sand — even when it had wandered away from its territory.

"The less I moved," Eugenie says, "the more the razorfish accepted me. After a while, they lost all fear and came to take food from my fingers instead of pulling their lightning-fast disappearing act."

5. The Strange Razorfish

Eugenie has studied five kinds of razorfish in the Red Sea. The strangest of all is the rare jet-black razorfish.

The black fish is startling against the white sand. Instead of fleeing or diving into the sand when danger is near, it lifts its feathery dorsal fin. It lies on its side and drifts in the current. It's hard to believe it's a living fish and not just a dark, drifting leaf.

Eugenie thinks that the black razorfish may imitate the black feather starfish. Feather starfish come in many colors. A feather starfish usually has five feathery arms rolled into a ball.

When a black feather starfish unrolls one of its arms, it looks very much like a black razorfish.

Schools of jack and tuna swoop down to pick off razorfishes. But they always leave the feather starfish and the black razorfish alone.

6. Boom Boom and Friends

When Eugenie studies a group of sand perch, she soon can tell each male fish apart. She looks at the different designs of stripes on their faces and can tell which one is Boom Boom or Fast Freddie or Mr. T. or Charlie or Uncle Albert. The volunteers who study the sand perch with Eugenie have fun naming the fish.

The females and babies don't have striped designs on their faces. They have spots, like polka dots.

The sand perch is a curious fish. If you swim into its territory, it will prop itself up with its two front fins resting on the sand and watch you. It will keep one eye on you facing forward, while the other eye looks sideways. Its two eyes can swivel in any direction — even completely backwards.

The sand perch, like the razorfish, live in harems. One male sand perch may live with two or three females.

7. Is It a Girl? Is It a Boy?

The sand perch, razorfish, and the sand tilefish can all change from female to male. Other fish make these changes, too.

It may sound confusing to you, but for a fish it can be a matter of life and death.

Fish that live in the desert beneath the sea are exposed to all kinds of danger from other fish. Even if they build burrows, they are mostly out in the open. There is no coral reef to hide in.

In this open, sandy area, it is the job of the male fish to protect his family. If something happens to the big male fish, then the next biggest fish in the family — a female — turns into a male. The complete change takes about two weeks. The new male becomes the protector. It is the job of the smaller females to produce the eggs.

Some fish make the opposite change, from male to female, like the clownfishes that live around the edges of the sandy desert. Big female clownfishes produce lots of eggs. When a female is injured or eaten or grows too old to lay eggs, a smaller male clownfish becomes female and produces eggs instead of sperm.

Male clownfishes don't have to be big protectors because they live in a large *anemone*. The anemone has stinging cells that keep bigger fish away.

8. An Octopus with Horns

You are swimming along when you see a funny-looking rock on the sand.

But wait! That funny-looking rock is actually a head with horns belonging to an octopus that lives in the sand.

If you stay very still, the octopus might extend one of its long arms, called *tentacles*, and grab your hand! The octopus develops startling striped rings around its tentacles when it reaches out to you.

If you move suddenly, the octopus will begin to sink into the sand.

Scientists do not know too much about the little sand octopus that is so rare and seems to live alone. Eugenie has seen only two. How do they find each other in the wide, wide world of sand?

9. Tricky Niki

Once Eugenie Clark was diving in the Red Sea. Her six-year-old son, Niki, was snorkeling above her. Eugenie looked down and saw a pointed nose in the sand. Then she saw two tiny eyes sticking out of the sand, watching her.

She kept very still. Soon a fish came out of the sand, a fish she had never seen before. It was shaped like an arrow. It lifted beautiful streamers behind its head, like a fan.

When she came closer, it lowered its "fan," shot headfirst into the sand, and disappeared.

Eugenie wondered if she would ever see this rare fish again. Maybe she had even imagined the whole thing. But she thought she would try an experiment, just in case.

Quickly she put a net over the sand where the fish had dived. With her free hand, she poked the sand around it. The experiment worked! The fish jumped up into the net and Eugenie had caught a new species.

When she came out of the water, her son Niki said, "Put the fish in my face mask, Mom." And together they carried it to the aquarium in the city of Eilat in Israel.

She named the fish *Trichonotus nikii*, after her son. *Trichonotus* refers to the long rays of its fan. *Trichonotus* is hard to say, so Eugenie and her diving friends call the fish Tricky Niki.

Eugenie was eager to see another Tricky Niki. Her friend David Fridman ran the aquarium. One day he said, "I have found a surprise for you." He took her to an out-of-the-way bay. Fish scientists, called *ichthyologists*, had not yet been to this bay. When Eugenie and David swam out a short distance, they saw an unbelievable sight—thousands of Tricky Nikis, swarming above the sand and feeding on *plankton*, tiny creatures drifting through the water.

Eugenie studied the Tricky Nikis. She saw that the male puts on a show to attract a female. Like a peacock spreading its plumes, he lifts his fan — the three striped plumes — above his body. He stiffens his body and makes himself look strong.

He also uses this display to scare away small fish.

10. The Odd Couple: The Shrimp and the Goby

A small goby, a fish less than six inches long, guards the entrance to a burrow built in the sand. It shares its home with a bulldozer shrimp that is nearly blind.

The small goby and the nearly blind shrimp need each other in the desert beneath the sea. Animals that help each other have a *symbiotic* relationship.

The bulldozer shrimp uses its big claws to bulldoze out the sand that keeps falling into their home. As the shrimp works, it keeps one of its feelers, called an *antenna*, on the goby's body.

The goby usually stands guard, as still as a statue. But if the goby senses danger, it vibrates its body. The shrimp's antenna picks up the vibration. That's the signal for the shrimp to disappear down the hole, with the goby following quickly after.

11. The Slinky Garden Eels

At first glance, these strange creatures look like dainty dancers. But though they sway to and fro in the current, their tails are always anchored in a hole in the sandy floor of the sea.

Here the amazing garden eels spend their entire lives eating, fighting, and mating with eels around them.

They are called garden eels because they look like swaying plants in an undersea garden. With their bodies upright, they look like they are growing out of the sand, unlike all other eels.

If you were diving and you spotted a garden of eels, you would swim closer to get a better look at them. But the closer you got, the faster the shy eels would disappear, sinking tailfirst into snakelike burrows in the sand.

There are more than a dozen different species of garden eels around the world. For many years, Eugenie has studied them in Japan, the Indian Ocean, and the Caribbean. But her favorite place is the Red Sea.

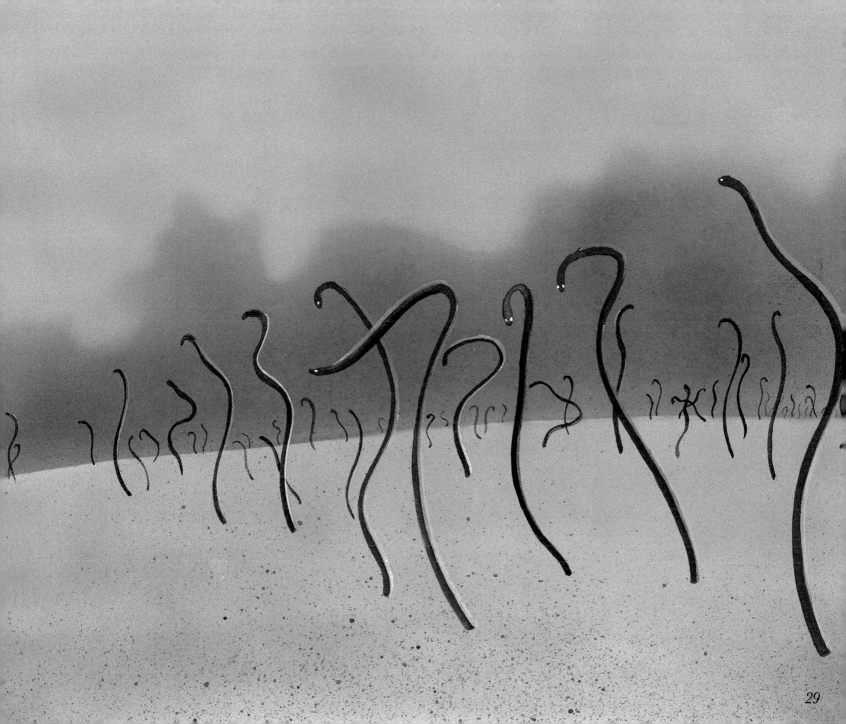

In order to study the eels up close, Eugenie has to hide so they won't be frightened and retreat into their burrows.

Using scuba gear, thirty feet below the surface, she enters a small enclosure, called a *blind*, set in the center of the eel colony. In time, the garden eels even get somewhat used to the divers.

Eugenie peers out of a peephole and sees hundreds of eels. Some are so close that she can look right into their eyes! They face into the gentle current, swaying from one side to another. They feed on fish eggs and other tiny creatures of the sea brought to them by the current.

She sees the male start courtship. He bends toward the female, rippling his long, white dorsal fin. Finally the pair of garden eels twist their bodies around each other, their tails still in the sand.

The eggs from this mating contain droplets of oil. The oil makes the eggs float. The current carries the eggs high and far away from their parents.

Eugenie studies the eels around the clock. Before sunrise, most of the eels rise from their burrows. At first only their heads stick up, looking like tiny periscopes on top of a submarine. Little by little, they rise higher and higher. By the time the sun comes up, thousands and thousands of eels are swaying in the sea, but the tips of their tails always stay in the sand.

Around noon, the colony begins to sink into the sand for a "*siesta*." Then a few hours later they rise up high again.

With time-lapse photography, a camera clicks a picture every hour, so Eugenie gets her sleep and her pictures at the same time. Not much goes on at night, though. The garden eels "sleep," too, staying in their burrows all through the night.

One of Eugenie's students, Phyllis Anastos, wanted to see how deep garden eels go into the sand and if they ever move their burrows. But how do you tag a slim garden eel that disappears at the first sight of you? Phyllis was able to tag a garden eel with David Fridman's help. He knew that the best way to get an eel out is to squirt an anesthetic down its burrow. When the groggy eel came out from its burrow, Phyllis tagged it with a bit of colored cork fastened to the eel with fine thread.

When the eel backed down into the sand, it made a new burrow and disappeared — but only two inches of the thread went down into the sand. This tagging experiment showed that eels hide just under the surface.

Phyllis and Eugenie laid a grid of string on the sand and mapped the exact location of each burrow opening within the grid.

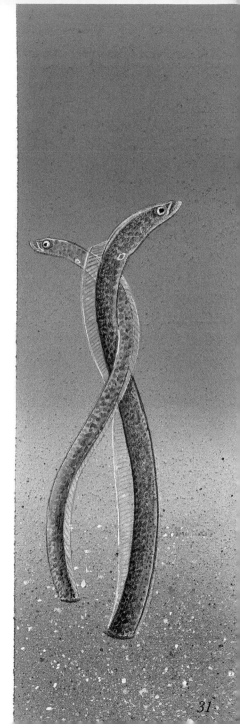

In a few days, they checked their map. They found that some of the holes were in a new location.

In time-lapse photos, a male was seen courting a female from his burrow. He was a foot away from the female's burrow. In the next photo, taken an hour later, he was only a few inches away from her!

So garden eels are not permanently planted. They do move, though no one has actually ever seen them do it!

Many questions still remain to be answered. To get to this new spot, does the male swim? Or does he tunnel through the sand? Why would a female move? Baby eels hatch high in the current and travel great distances. How do the baby eels find their way back to their parents' colony? Or do they join another colony?

Eugenie says that when the garden eels face into a strong current, they look like question marks swaying in the sea. The question marks tell her that there are still unsolved puzzles about these fascinating creatures.

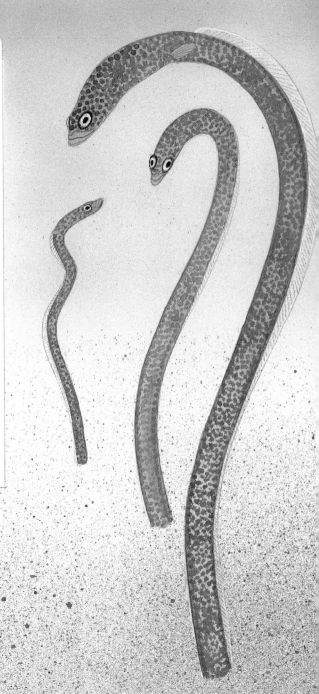

12. The Mighty Moses Sole

The sand-dwelling Moses sole looks like a small flounder in a fish market.

The first time Eugenie caught the Moses sole in the Red Sea, some milky-white fluid oozed out along its fins when she grabbed it. The milky stuff felt slimy and her fingers felt tingly! She wondered if the fish was poisonous.

Eugenie tested the Moses sole with a shark in the lab. When she put the little fish in the shark tank, the shark opened its jaws wide to gobble it up. But the shark's jaws stayed stuck open! It began thrashing and leaping about the tank, shaking its head wildly from side to side. The Moses sole didn't have a scratch on it. It had kept the shark from closing its jaws.

Then Eugenie washed the skin of the Moses sole with alcohol. Once more, she dropped the fish in the shark tank and in no time the Moses sole was gobbled up. She learned that washing the fish with alcohol took away the poison in the mucous on its skin. Cooking also destroyed all its poison. A cooked Moses sole is safe to eat and tastes good, too.

Eugenie wondered how sharks in the sea would react to the Moses sole. Volunteers set out shark lines, over deep water. They baited the line with ten different fish. Only one was the Moses sole.

Night came. It was the hour for sharks to be active.

Eugenie and a volunteer entered the calm sea. Suddenly the

water rippled over the shark line. A dark shadow drifted up from the deep. Then another and another! Silently and swiftly, sharks swam near to the little Moses sole wriggling on the line. But then the sharks turned away!

The sharks ate up all the fish one by one — all but the Moses sole!

Eugenie had discovered a fish that is a shark repellent. A thimbleful of the Moses sole's poisonous fluid can keep hungry sharks away for many hours.

Other scientists began studying the Moses sole and its poison. They put a small shark in a tank along with the fluid from one Moses sole. In six hours, the shark was dead!

A company that makes suntan lotions heard about the Moses sole. The company had made a suntan lotion that doesn't come off in the water. Now they wanted to make a product that prevented sunburn *and* shark attack — all in one tube.

There is another chemical in the milky fluid of the Moses sole. This chemical can block the poison of bees, scorpions, and poisonous snakes. Eugenie hopes that research might lead to a way to help save lives.

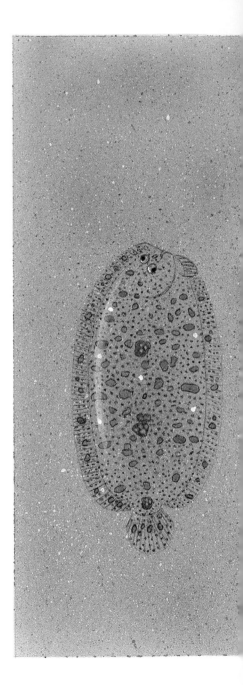

13. Long-nose Sea Moths

Usually these rare creatures move sluggishly along the sandy bottom. You can't see them unless they make a move. And when they stop moving, they blend so well into their sandy background that they seem to disappear in front of your eyes.

By a fast wiggling of their tails, they lift off from the bottom. Then they glide on winglike fins, "flying" in short spurts. They'll even land on your outstretched hand if you lie quietly.

The smaller male follows the female, perhaps to court her. The female is larger and carries a "basket" of eggs in her body.

These little sea moths are only four inches long. They are relatives of the sea horses and have the same hard covering, called an *exoskeleton*. A sea moth can shed the outer layer of its body in one piece, like a snake shedding its skin. This layer looks like a sea moth ghost.

Eugenie's student, Daphna Herold, tags sea moths in the Red Sea. She puts a tiny disc with a number on it near the sea moth's tail. She wants to keep track of them in the sand where they are so hard to find. She found one ten days after it was tagged and released.

These fish are sometimes called Pegasus, named for the flying winged horse of ancient fairy tales.

In China and other parts of the Far East, some people still make a tea of ground-up sea moths. They say it's a cure for sore throats.

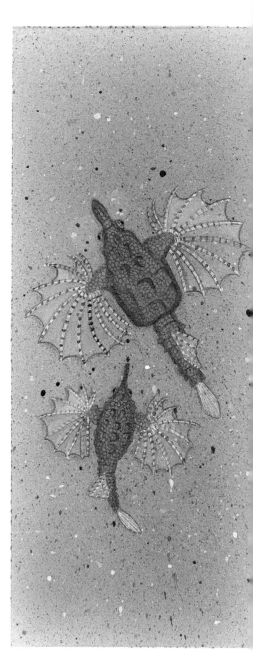

14. A Nasty Mouthful

Most snails are protected by their hard shells. But this dark six-inch snail — a sea slug — doesn't have a shell.

It is easy to see on the sand, so it needs something else to protect it.

Its protection is its terrible taste! Its enemies spit it out. The nasty taste comes from a chemical in the coating of the sea slug.

A tiny shrimp makes its home on the sea slug. Scientists are not sure why. Perhaps the shrimp feeds on parasites on the skin of the sea slug. Perhaps it is an easy and safe way for the shrimp to travel around.

When two sea slugs find each other to mate, their two symbiotic shrimp can also find each other.

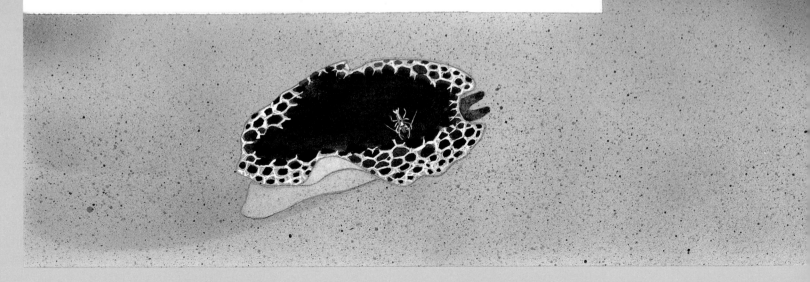

15. Lionfish: A Poisonous Beauty

Beautiful lionfish like to cuddle up to you on the sand. But be careful! Their dorsal fins are tipped with poisonous toxins!

When lionfish cross the sand, they look for a good place to hide so they can pounce on some unsuspecting fish, such as a poor Tricky Niki caught off guard.

So if you're lying on the sandy bottom, quietly making observations, the lionfish might think that you're as good a hiding place as a sunken log. You could end up with half a dozen lionfish tucked around you, hiding under your shadow in the sand.

If you find yourself with lionfish around you, you mustn't startle them. Just move slowly and gently away.

16. Jumping Sand Grains

You look down at the sandy floor of the undersea desert and suddenly see sand grains jumping around like crazy.

Actually there are tiny, tiny creatures hiding under the sand grains. They stick together bits of shells and grains of sand to build a tiny "house," which they carry along as they hop. The creatures themselves are transparent and only as big as small green peas in a pod. You can't see them. You can only see their hopping "houses."

Carol Falck, one of Eugenie's students, has been studying the jumping sand grains in the Red Sea. She is the first person to observe a "house" with "rooms" for a mother and her ten babies.

Carol collects the creatures and their houses in glass tubes. She looks at them under a microscope. Each little house has one pair of wings and a rear room made out of a tiny shell in which still another creature lives. Carol discovered that the stranger in the house is a new species, not even related to the others.

Why is the stranger there? Carol plans other trips to the Red Sea to find out. She also wants to know how fast the creatures hop and why they hop. She thinks that so many jumping sand grains hopping at the same time might confuse a predator who wants to feed on just one creature.

Carol has problems studying the jumping sand grains. It's hard to mark something that small to keep track of it.

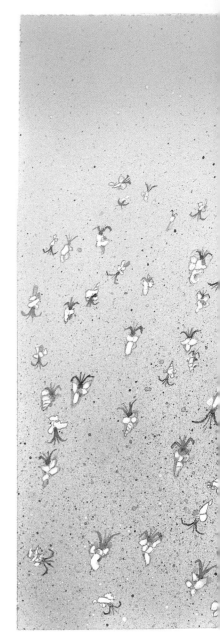

17. Strange Fish in the Sand

Pufferfish

Scuba divers love to play with pufferfish on a coral reef. Pufferfish can inflate themselves with water. They look like balloons with spines sticking out all over.

But the sand pufferfish is smooth. The fish can flatten their bellies and shovel their shoulders into the sand until they almost disappear and only their eyes stick out.

Goatfish

Goatfish have whiskers on their chins. Their whiskers have taste buds like you have on your tongue.

Goatfish poke their whiskers into the sand to search for worms and other little creatures. When they taste something good to eat, their whole nose goes into the sand and stirs up the tasty treats. Smaller fish swim above the goatfish and swoosh down to the sand to feed on what the goatfish has stirred up.

Stingray

Stingrays can bury themselves in the sand, except for two eyes and two big breathing openings, called *spiracles*. If you step on a buried stingray by accident, it will defend itself. It can whip up its tail and its sharp spine can give you a painful wound.

Panther Flounder

The panther flounder is a relative of the Moses sole. Flounders and soles lie flat on the sand, but not on their bellies. They lie down on one side or the other. The panther flounder can change the color of its upper side to match its background. When it swims over sand, it turns as white as the sand. Sometimes it has bright blue spots, like the design on a peacock's fanlike tail.

Crocodile Fish

The crocodile fish is related to the lionfish but it's not poisonous. It has a big flat head and looks a bit like a crocodile. This fish lies quietly in the sand, waiting for its prey. It doesn't wiggle into the sand. Instead, it uses camouflage to hide its big body — sometimes three feet long. It blends into the sand so well you can't even tell it's there.

Sand Burrower

In some parts of the sand there are more than 50 tiny transparent fish in one square yard. They hide just under the sand. They never swim. They jump out of the sand so quickly that you can hardly believe something moved when you poked the sand.

There are still many questions scientists want to know about these strange fishes that live in the desert beneath the sea.

18. A Mystery Fish

One day, Eugenie and her friend David Shen were diving in the Red Sea. They were studying razorfish when David noticed a strange fish swimming by. David had never seen such a fish before.

It looked like a tiny jawfish with a big head and four dark patches on its back. It was a female with her belly bulging with eggs. He took many pictures of the fish.

David motioned to Eugenie. She swam over to the mystery fish. She, too, had never seen anything like it. They collected it in a plastic bag and brought it to the surface. They kept it alive in a bucket of seawater and brought it to David Fridman at the aquarium. Surely he would be able to identify the fish.

But David Fridman didn't know what it was, either. By chance, a

scientist from a museum in Germany happened to be visiting the Red Sea. He got very excited when he saw the strange little fish and asked to take it back to his museum.

It turned out to be a new species. He preserved the fish by pickling it in a jar with special chemicals. He described it in a scientific paper and named it *Stalix davidsheni*, after David Shen.

David Shen says today, "I often wonder what that little fish was doing, swimming over the sand. It was not the usual jawfish behavior. Jawfish usually build their burrows in sand and rubble. They almost never wander far from their homes. Was this rare fish looking for its mate?"

Since that day in 1984, no other *Stalix davidsheni* has been seen, but Eugenie and David keep looking.

David Shen joined Eugenie and Ann McGovern on a Red Sea trip in 1980 because he wanted to learn about fish. It was his first expedition. Since then he has become an expert underwater photographer, and some of his pictures have been on magazine covers.

David has also become an expert on many kinds of fish. He became fascinated with the desert beneath the sea and produced a movie about it. He helped Eugenie map the largest colony of garden eels in the world. He knows fish by their scientific names.

If you help scientists, like David does, perhaps some day, you, too, will have a fish named after you!

19. Riddles of the Sea

You've met some of the creatures of the desert beneath the sea. You've learned their habits and found out how scientists study them.

There are still many mysteries to be explored, questions to be answered, and solutions to be found.

In years to come, scientists will find many answers to unsolved riddles of the sea.

Maybe one of the scientists will be you.

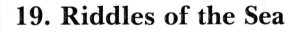

45

INDEX

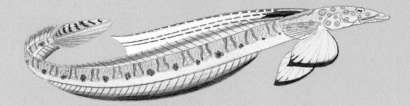

Goatfish	*Pseudopeneus forsskali* (Say: sood o PEN ee us for SKA lee)	40
Goby	*Amblyeleotris sungami* (Say: am blee el ee O tris sun GAM ee)	27
Jack	*Caranx* (Say: KA ranx)	21
Jawfish	*Stalix davidsheni* (Say: STA lix da vid SHEN ee)	42–43

Jumping sand grains:

gypsy amphipod (crustacean)	*Siphonocetes erythraeus* (Say: see fon o CEE tees a RITH ree us)	38–39
copepod stranger	*Ellucana* (Say: el loo CAN a)	38–39
Lionfish	*Pterois radiata* (Say: TER oys ray dee A ta)	37
Moses sole	*Pardachirus marmoratus* (Say: par da KY rus mar mor AY tus)	33–34,41
Panther flounder	*Bothus pantherinus* (Say: BO thus pan ther EYE nus)	41
Plankton	(There are many species of plankton.)	26
Pufferfish	*Arothron hispidus* (Say: A roth ron HIS pid us)	40

Razorfish	*Xyrichtys pentadactylus*	18–19,22,
	(Say: zer IK tus pen ta DAC ty lis)	23,42
Sand burrower	*Limnichthys nitidus*	41
	(Say: lim NIK thees NYE tye dus)	
Sand octopus	*Octopus* (species)	24
	(SAY: OK to pus)	
Sand perch	*Parapercis hexophthalma*	22,23
	(Say: par ra PUR sis hex of THAL ma)	
Sand tilefish	*Malacanthus plumieri*	12–17,23
	(Say: mal a CAN thus ploo mee ER ee)	
Sea moth	*Eurypegasus draconis*	35
	(Say: ur ee PEG a sis dra CONE us)	
Sea slug	*Pleurobranchus* (species)	36
	(Say: pler o BRANK us)	
Shark	*Triaenodon obesus*	33–34
	(SAY: try EEN o don o BAY ses)	
Stingray	*Taeniura lymma*	40,41
	(Say: tee nee UR a LIM ma)	
Symbiotic shrimp	*Periclimenes imperator*	36
	(Say: per ee CLYE men ness im per A tor)	
Tricky Niki	*Trichonotus nikii*	25–26,37
	(Say: try ko NO tus NIK kee eye)	
Tuna	*Thunnus*	21
	(Say: TUN us)	